The Path
TO EMOTIONAL
HEALING
BE HAPPY LIVING NOW

ROBERT MOMENT

LEGAL STATEMENT

The Path to Emotional Healing

Copyright © 2010 by Robert Moment.

All rights reserved.

No part of this book may be used or reproduced in any manner without the express written permission of the author.

ISBN-13: 978-0-9799982-7-0

LIABILITY/WARRANTY

The views and interpretations expressed in this book are the authors, and are not intended to provide exact or specific advice. The author shall not be liable for any loss or damage incurred in the process of following advice presented in this book.

Limit of Liability/Disclaimer of Warranty: While the publisher and the author have used their best efforts in preparing this book, they make no representations or warranties with respect to the accuracy or completeness of the contents of this book and specifically disclaim any implied warranties of merchantability or fitness for a particular purpose. No warranty may be created or extended by sales representatives or written sales materials. The advice and strategies contained herein may not be suitable for your situation. You should consult with a professional where appropriate. If medical, psychological or any other expert assistance is required, the services of a competent professional person should be sought. Neither the publisher nor the author shall be liable for any loss or profit or any other commercial damages, including but not limited to special, incidental, consequential, or other damages. In summary this book is not a substitute for professional healthcare and advice.

All Scripture quotations and references are from the following sources:

Holy Bible, New Living Translation (NLT), © 1996, 2004. Used by permission of Tyndale House Publishers, Inc, Wheaton, Illinois 60189. All rights reserved.

Holy Bible, Today's New International Version (TNIV) Copyright 2001, 2005 by Biblica. All rights reserved worldwide.

New International Version (NIV) Holy Bible, New International Version, Copyright 1973 1978, 1984 Biblica. Used by permission of Zondervan . All rights reserved.

The New King James Version. © 1982 by Thomas Nelson, Inc. Used by permission. All rights reserved.

21st Century King James Version, copyright © 1994. Used by permission of Deuel Enterprises, Inc. Gary, SD 57237. All rights reserved.

The Good News Bible: The Bible in Today's English Version (TEV), American Bible Society: New York, © 1976.

Special Prayer for You
A New Beginning

Dear Heavenly Father,

Thanks for loving me just as I am. I choose to recognize my worth in You. I praise You for being everything I need in my life. Thank you for taking extra-special care of me. Thank you for wrapping your arms around me and holding me close to You. Thank you for your grace, mercy, favor and love. Every day is a new day of healing and promise being in Your presence.

I accept it and give thanks for the new path and plan You have for my life.

I choose faith over fear and trust over doubt. Give me wisdom daily to seek You first above all things. Remind me to turn to You first for all the answers I need. Father, I trust You completely with my past, present and future.

I celebrate being Your precious gift for I am chosen... I am blessed. I love you, Father.

Every day I choose to rest in Your care knowing that You are more than enough.

Thank you for Your strength every day and hope for tomorrow.

In the Name of Jesus,
Amen.

–Robert Moment

Table of Contents

Introduction 1
A New Mind Shift 5
Opening Up and Letting Go 21
The Healing Power of Forgiveness 33
Choose to Be Free from Your Past 47
Discovering Your Divine Purpose Leads to Happiness 59
Speaking Positive Life-Changing Words 71
Celebrate Your Uniqueness 81
The Power of Giving 87
Happiness is an Inside Job 93
Be Happy Living How 97
One Final Thought 103

Introduction

If you are ready to experience emotional healing, you can begin right now. You don't have to suffer in "silence" alone. How much is it costing (living a life of happiness) you to remain in "silence" ? Now is the time to "break your silence" and walk the Path to Emotional Healing and Find Happiness Again in your life. Open your heart to the possibilities that only God can bring. *Your life matters to God.* Step into the flow of God's love and live a life of happiness forever. Yes, I did say forever.

Have you ever been hurt, betrayed, rejected or abandoned? Is there any hurt or pain in your life that you have not addressed? How has that pain affected your life? How about your relationships? Are you struggling with feelings of anger, resentment, fear or doubt towards yourself or others? Are you happy with yourself right now?

Do any of these questions strike a chord in your heart? If so, you can find the answers you are looking for inside this power-packed life transforming book to "break your silence". You will find solutions for mastering your emotions and emotional healing. This inspirational happiness guide book will show you step by step "how to" walk the Path to Emotional Healing and Find Happiness Again:

The Path to Emotional Healing

- How to Open up and Let go of Your painful memories
- How to Master Your Emotions
- The Healing Power of Forgiveness
- 6 Powerful Steps on How to Forgive Others for Emotional Healing (Closure)
- 6 Powerful Steps on How to Forgive Yourself for Emotional Healing (Closure)
- How to Celebrate Your Uniqueness
- How to gain Spiritual Growth and Power
- 7 Steps on How to Discover YOUR life's purpose
- Learn the Power of Speaking positive life-changing words
- Why Happiness comes from the way You feel inside

Transformation in life always starts with small principles applied in powerful ways. This life-changing book is the bridge to a brand new beginning in your life. Don't ever give up on yourself or your life.

God has great things in store for you. If you don't believe me, keep reading. By the time you finish this book, you will believe it to. Why? Because God will use His all-encompassing power to show you things about Himself and you that were previously not known.

You will laugh, cry and scream at times, but there won't ever be a time that God isn't right there to take it all in. Don't worry – His shoulders are broad enough and His arms long

Introduction

and strong enough to hold you and handle whatever you have to tell Him.

You'll have to be patient with yourself as you read this life-changing emotional healing and happiness book. Be gentle with yourself. Dare to be vulnerable. Be open to " profound change" and a "new beginning" by telling the truth about what you are feeling, the truth about what you are thinking, the truth about what you are doing and the truth about why you are doing it. It is only when you tell the truth about yourself that emotional healing begins.

Honor the healing process with patience and faith. Through it, you will be able to let go of painful memories that have kept you trapped for years or your entire life. You'll discover how much more there is to living life and being happy once those things are gone.

I wrote this book to give you real life expert advice that you can actually use on how you can forgive, heal yourself emotionally and live a life of happiness. Choose to Be Happy Now. You are a "Gift" to this world. There is so much value inside of YOU. Every life can experience a New Beginning.

In writing this emotional healing and happiness book it is my sincere hope to offer you support and guidance if you are experiencing or have experienced emotional pain and hurt in your life. I've experienced emotional pain and hurt in my life. No one is exempt from it. Life can really hurt sometimes and we feel so burden down by the pain and disappointment.

The Path to Emotional Healing

Don't *ever* "give in" or "give up" on life. Let's *agree* in *prayer* that you will be healed from your emotional pain and hurt. Affirm your healing in belief and faith. Say out loud- *I am healed, And so it is, In Jesus Name, Amen.*

> *"He sent out his word and healed them."*
> –Psalm 107:20

You can get through it. I didn't say it would be easy. No matter what category of pain and hurt you are in I want to share with you the most effective path to emotional healing and happiness.

Are there painful circumstances, situations or relationships in your life that you have been struggling to overcome or trying to work through ? You don't have to live your life like this. Refuse to accept that this is just the way life is. I am happy to say that this emotional healing book is for you. I am so grateful to be able to support you and to serve you as you undertake this life-changing journey toward a life of emotional healing and happiness.

You can be happy again in life no matter what has happened in the past. Happiness is a choice. May God Bless You Richly!

A New Mind Shift

Pain, although uncomfortable, is not a permanent state. When you are in the midst of an emotional situation, it may seem that way, but God assures us that we will overcome it. You can't do it alone. You need Him by your side at every turn. How about it? Will you take God along?

What does this mean for you? It requires a mind shift – "Change Your Thinking and Change Your Life."

> *"Instead, let the Spirit renew your thoughts and attitudes."*
>
> *–Ephesians 4:23*

Renewing your mind is a lifelong process. It begins with taking your thoughts captive. Round them up in one place in your mind and have a good look at them. What are they telling you: *I am too far gone? I am "damaged goods"? I am a loser? I don't look good enough? I am "too old"? I can't do anything right? I deserve what I got?*

These are all mind tricks of the enemy, lies that he would have us believe to keep us in emotional bondage and unhappy. The mind is the most important battlefield in our lives and Satan knows that. If he loses here, he has lost you forever.

God can help you renew your mind day by day. Let's examine our thoughts from His perspective: *Who does God say that you are? What does He say that you can do? What does He say about your future happiness?* Now, who are you going to believe? See yourself from God's perspective. Your *story* will end in *victory*. God will *always* give you the *victory*.

A major part of emotional pain is grief. Grief doesn't just follow death but any type of loss. It is also a part of the natural healing process. You may not think so as you try to go about your everyday routine, with no success. The sorrow and confusion can be devastating.

There is no time frame for your hurt and pain, but you can get stuck in a rut. No matter what you do, nothing ever seems to get better.

There are experts who have broken down the stages of grief into five categories:

1. Stage One: Denial
2. Stage Two: Pain
3. Stage Three: Anger
4. Stage Four: Depression
5. Stage Five: Acceptance

While these five stages are an excellent way to gauge whether you are moving forward, there is another way to look at your pain and to learn how to handle it – a three-part process of *meeting it, managing it* and *mastering it*. These three phases allow you to process the hurt in your life in clear, concise ways that enable you to move forward with God's help.

Meeting Your Pain and Hurt

The first step is often the hardest. You feel like you are stepping off into the unknown. *What will happen once the floodgates are open?* The truth of the matter is it can't be any worse than what you are dealing with right now.

Right now, when you look in the mirror, you see a stranger staring back at you. Your family wonders why you are still "out of it." Depending on the cause of your pain, it may be years after the event has occurred. Ignoring the problem has placed a suffocating bandage over it that has only served to spread the infection throughout your life. There are periods of time when you feel fine, but you revert back to that unhappy state every time.

Sometimes we deny hurt and pain in our lives for many months or even years rather than meeting and acknowledging them. Examples of loss like this include: loss of trust (betrayal by a loved one), loss of love , loss of marriage(divorce) or a spouse (death), loss of virginity, loss of security, loss of acceptance, loss of friendship, loss of innocence (physical, sexual, verbal or psychological abuse), loss of education, loss of a child or loss of employment.

What does denial look like? When emotional pain threatens to overtake us, some of the signs are: depression, attitude changes, anger, jealousy, and even paranoia. You want to behave differently but it seems almost impossible. That's the power that pain and hurt has over you until you take control and take back your ability to live a happy life.

Are you ready for a *new* chapter in your life? If you are tired of living on an emotional rollercoaster, listen up. You can't cope properly unless you are able to face your demons (for that is what they truly are) head-on, accepting them for what they are and how they are impacting your life. It's time to let God in on your pain.

Who is God?

Who is God you say? You aren't the first person to ask aloud or wonder silently. When we are feeling the emotional pains that can accompany any life, there will be someone who says "Pray to God." It may be a knee-jerk reaction to the situation, like a death in the family or talking about emotional events of the past. But, somewhere inside, they knew to mention His name. They may have forgotten how, but that person, and maybe even you, knows that God can help.

So, here are a few facts about the power of God and just how good He is:

A New Mind Shift

The power of God is unlimited and, in its vastness, unknowable in all its forms, yet this amazing and vast power gives us hope and should give us the confidence to go forward in life without fear. Think about the infinite power of God – He is the One who rolls back the clouds and brings forth sunshine after a storm. He orders the winds to blow and creates the seasons in order to bring forth food on the earth and provide for all the creatures on it. We can rely on the fact that night follows day and winter is followed by spring because God's power makes it so. See, you can't help but smile when you think about it.

In fact, God is unique in the entire universe in His power. He has attributes that no one and nothing else has that demonstrate the infinite variety and omniscience of His power:

- **No other creature is capable of creation from nothing.** God alone created the universe itself and all the creatures in it. He created night and day, the planets and stars and everything on the earth that sustains life. He willed the very universe into existence and existed before it came into being.

- **No other creature is self-sustaining like God is.** Plants require water and light, animals and people require food. God requires nothing – He simply IS, with nothing else required.

- **No other creature can forgive like God can forgive.** While we can forgive others for harm they may have done to us, no one has the ability to forgive us all of our transgressions and grant absolution – giving us hope of eternal life.

- **No other creature is Infinite.** He was here at the beginning of time, and is outside of time. In fact, God and His son, Jesus Christ, *are* the beginning and the end, the Alpha and Omega of the universe.

"In the beginning was the Word, and the Word was with God, and the Word was God. He was with God in the beginning. Through Him all things were made. In Him was life, and that life was the light of men."
—*John 1:1-4*

So who or what should we put our faith in? The power of kingdoms and men will fade away, but God is eternal. He is like nothing and no one else and can be relied on for all your needs. Do you fully realize and understand the power of His presence in your life? Many believers speak of the acts of God on a large scale, but have you ever considered the amazing power of His presence in your own life, the personal power that you have by giving your life over to Him?

The next time you are fearful or do not know where to turn, remember that the most powerful force on earth and in heaven is God. He doesn't have to do anything but be there, and you'll have all you need at your disposal to overcome anything through Him.

A New Mind Shift

"For nothing will be impossible with God."
—Luke 1:37

Praying for God's help as you face your pain will give you the strength to accept what has happened to you and understand that you have the strength, with His love, to survive and find happiness. There are many different kinds of circumstances that cause the heart to ache and shatter. Regardless of what they are, you must be able to meet them and look them square in the face and be able to embrace it, if not willingly, at least realistically.

When you are ready to let go of the festering pain that these losses are causing you, pray to the Lord and He will help you with the face-to-face meeting. You will need to take that time to properly mourn. You may cry for a while, or spend some time alone or talk with someone who understands your pain. Whatever you need to do to allow the pain to be washed away is fine. At that point, you have taken the first step toward overcoming your pain and hurt.

Enhance Your Prayer Experience - The 7 Steps of Prayer

Many people get anxious when you talk about prayer. They envision the preacher in the pulpit using "thee" and "thou" in his prayer over the congregation. Prayer is simply a conversation with God. He doesn't require fancy language and terms that we have heard before but don't even know the meaning of.

In Philippians, chapter 4, verses 6 and 7, Paul tells us to take everything to God in prayer:

> *"Do not be anxious about anything, but in everything, by prayer and petition, with thanksgiving, present your requests to God. And the peace of God, which transcends all understanding, will guard your hearts and your minds in Christ Jesus."*

What a promise this is! We just have to pray about our hurt, we just have to take our broken hearts to God, and he will replace our pain with peace. If the whole world knew this, wouldn't we be spending most of our time on our knees? It is a peace that transcends our understanding. That is a peace that sounds even stronger than my pain.

God desires sincerity from us. When you talk to Him, speak with respect like you were talking to a parent or someone older than you but also talk plainly like you would to a friend or a loved one. After all, God is your Heavenly Father, your friend and your brother.

When you spend time with the Lord, don't ask Him where He is, because He is always there, right beside you. Instead, ask the Lord questions that can help you learn and grow as one of His children. Ask God, "What should I do, Lord, to

A New Mind Shift

face these difficulties? What do you want me to learn from my hurt? Will you help me to be strong in Your love and find happiness in my life?" Remember to walk in faith and ask God the right questions, He will answer in that still, soft voice in the night that comforts you just when you thought He wasn't there.

The world may attack us, but with God we will not be defeated. We may struggle a bit, but God will never abandon us. We may be brought low, but we will never be crushed under the weight – because God is always there.

> *"The Lord is near to all who call on Him,*
> *to all who call on Him in truth.*
> *He fulfills the desires of those who fear him;*
> *He hears their cry and saves them.*
> *The Lord watches over all who love Him."*
> *–Psalm 145:18-20*

In, God we have unparalleled hope and courage. God is the One Presence, the One Power in the universe.

God taught His disciples how to pray in the Sermon on the Mount. You probably know it as the Lord's Prayer. You learned it as a child. Now, read it slowly and really take in what it says about prayer.

[7] *"When you pray, don't babble on and on as people of other religions do. They think their prayers are answered merely by*

repeating their words again and again. ⁸ Don't be like them, for your Father knows exactly what you need even before you ask him! ⁹ Pray like this:

> *Our Father in heaven,*
> *may your name be kept holy.*
> *¹⁰ May your Kingdom come soon.*
> *May your will be done on earth,*
> *as it is in heaven.*
> *¹¹ Give us today the food we need,*
> *¹² and forgive us our sins,*
> *as we have forgiven those who sin against us.*
> *¹³ And don't let us yield to temptation,*
> *but rescue us from the evil one."*
>
> *–Matthew 6:7-13*

It will take some time to get used to. God doesn't mind if you practice. He wants to talk to you – always. Here are seven steps to help you learn to pray effectively.

1. **Acknowledge your personal relationship with God.** You are His child and can come into His presence (speak to Him) at any time. What do you tell your parents? Tell God how much you love Him and want to get to know Him. Praise God during prayer and throughout your day, becoming absorbed in Him. This makes God happy.

2. **Acknowledge your respect for who God is.** Recognizing that God is holy and powerful, give Him the reve-

rence that He deserves, meaning, show respect. Let Him know that you believe in His power to do just what He says He will do. Whatever you need, He can provide. Commit your life to God each day, promising to live according to His will.

3. **Confess your sins.** It is so important to ask God to forgive your sins. We all make mistakes whether we are living for God or not. Asking God to come into your life won't stop the mistakes. We are still human. But, it does help us to realize how little we can do without Him. Repentance is a sign of your understanding that you have – like all of us have – broken God's commands, and are sorry for what you have done. By acknowledging that our sins have separated us temporarily from God, we are once again brought closer to Him.

4. **Ask God for His help in prayer.** Many of us feel guilty if we ask God for anything, fearing that we aren't worthy and that we are being demanding, or that we might anger God. It is just the opposite – by asking God, we are acknowledging that we can't do it alone; we are recognizing our need for His divine intervention and showing that we trust in Him to help us. Nothing could make God happier!

5. **Be specific in prayer.** Prayers can be quite general, asking for blessings from the Lord, but it is okay to be specific, too. When we ask the Lord to help us find a better job, resolve a problem with our spouse or anything

else that is personal to us, we are opening our innermost hearts to Him. This personal, private kind of prayer asking for specific help tells God that we have faith in Him to watch over us in small ways as well as big ones. He wants to be the Lord of our lives in all things large and small, so it is fine to pray to find a way to get a new dryer if yours breaks down!

6. **Have an attitude of expectancy and faith.** Trust that God can answer any prayer. Have faith that God will hear you when you pray according to His will. Now, praying according to His will means that we acknowledge that He will answer us in His time and His way. Do not pray in fear or out of desperation because "nothing else has worked." Pray confidently, with the faith that God will fulfill your expectations in the best way possible for you, born out of His divine wisdom.

> "Listen to me! You can pray for anything, and if you believe, you will have it."
>
> –Mark 11:24

7. **Pray in Jesus' name.** When we pray in Jesus' name, we enter into a relationship with Jesus Christ, God's own son. We are able to take full advantage of Jesus' death on the cross as a payment for our sins by acknowledging His sacrifice in our prayers. It also ties us to the new life of Christ's resurrection. The secret of our Christian life is also the secret of praying – doing all in Jesus' name.

A New Mind Shift

"Whatever you ask in my name, that I will do."
–John 14:13

Every prayer is important. Every prayer counts. Our prayers lift God up, showing others just who He is. There is power in prayer. In His presence, we will find our greatest blessings and the path to happiness again.

Managing Your Pain and Hurt

Managing your pain means understanding how to live your life and move forward with that pain as a part of the whole. The Lord will give you the strength to integrate your hurt into your daily living and learn how to slowly overcome the pain and depression that may have stopped you from moving forward before. Management is about being able to slowly let the normalcy of life back into your days and giving yourself permission to move on and live in happiness. When your life begins to feel familiar to you once again, you are on the right track.

Don't look for any quick fixes here though. God is not into fly-by-night solutions. It will take time. If you have fallen into a depression, God's answer for you may be medication to manage it and begin the healing process.

Mastering Your Pain and Hurt

Mastering your pain comes when you are able to move past it and overcome it. You do not have to forget the past or lose the memories of what has happened, but you *do* have to overcome the power that it has to hurt you. It is healthy to feel sad after a loss, but there comes a time for the mourning to end and new life to begin.

> *"There is a time for everything,*
> *and a season for every activity under heaven…*
> *a time to weep and a time to laugh,*
> *a time to mourn and a time to dance."*
> *—Ecclesiastes 3:1-4*

Survivor's guilt will try and prevent you from moving on. It's the shame we feel because we are still alive and our loved one is no longer with us. It happens when someone dies of an illness and also if there was some sort of accident and you made it but they didn't.

With other types of hurt, moving on can feel like a return to the denial stage. If you let the pain go, you are acting like the incident that caused the pain never happened or didn't mean anything. That couldn't be farther from the truth. God assures us that our lives are meant to have many different phases and nothing, including pain, is meant to last forever. He created a world that is meant to be a gift full of happiness and joy even when bad things happen.

A New Mind Shift

When you cope with pain, remember that the Lord is always listening and will be there to give you comfort and support. Pray for His help and you will find that the road toward meeting, managing and mastering your pain and hurt to be one you can travel with less sorrow and more joy than you would have expected.

The indwelling love of God is our source of inspiration for overcoming pain and hurt. Thank You, God, for Your presence of love, life and light.

Opening Up and Letting Go

"You will never truly know faith, yourself and God until you have been tested by adversity"
—Robert Moment

Remember those trust exercises you did for fun in school? You stood with your back to one person or the entire class. Then, you opened your arms and allowed yourself to fall freely backwards in hopes that someone would care enough to catch you. That is what God will do when you open up about your pain and trust Him enough to fall into His loving and capable arms. What do you have to lose except the emotional hurts that you've been carrying around?

You have already been introduced to prayer. As you continue to pray you will feel God talking back to you. It is amazing isn't it?

It is our nature to hold on to what has become familiar. For you, that will be your grief and the anger at your loss. Anger is a part of the grief process, but it is so much more than that. Holding on to the anger keeps the pain alive so we don't forget how badly we were hurt. Unfortunately, it also hinders God from entering every part of us and sharing His life-giving love. It is necessary to let go but we must first allow ourselves to open up and let go of it all.

God Can Heal You

When you were young and you hurt yourself playing, someone came along and cleaned it out and put a bandage on your wound. The cleaning hurt but once the bandage went on you knew that things would be better. And, you could wipe your tears and go back to playing.

You are older now and your hurts are bigger than any bandage could cover. That just means that you need the help of someone with better healing skills. That's where God comes in. Now, it will hurt when He cleans out the wounds but He will wipe the tears and allow you to get back to life. What are you waiting for?

You might know this in your head, but saying it out loud helps it to reach your heart. God is love. It's in the Bible. It's been said so many times that the words have almost lost their meaning. But if we meditate on the idea, it returns to its profound roots.

Love is the only cure for the devastating emotional wounds that we suffer. According to scripture, God has a soft spot for those who suffer. Psalm 34:18 reads, "The Lord is close to the brokenhearted, and saves those who are crushed in spirit." God knows how many hairs are on your head (Matthew

10:30). He knows the condition of your heart (Psalm 139). And, He cares about every second of your pain (1 Peter 5:7, John 3:16).

Realize that God cares about every part of who you are and that includes the bad as well as the good. His love is all-encompassing and can handle everything that we throw His way. Consider the story of Luke, chapter 8. It involves a woman who suffered from a blood issue for twelve long years and she was no further to finding a resolution than when she had begun, until she dared to meet Jesus.

Jesus was walking along and the crowds were pushing in on Him and almost crushing Him. All of a sudden he turned around and said, "Who touched me?" The disciples, a bit baffled, were like, well Lord, several hundred people are touching you, and Jesus said, "Someone touched me; I know that power has gone out of me." The woman who had grabbed at his cloak came forward and told Jesus how she had touched Him for healing and that she had already been healed. Jesus said to her, "Daughter, your faith has healed you. Go in peace."

Faith plays a big part in your emotional healing. Unless you believe in your heart that God can heal you, you are already fighting a losing battle. He wants you to need Him, and when you allow yourself to need Him, that's when the healing begins. You may no longer be a child, but God asks that you accept His words of promise in the Bible as a child would – at face value.

The Path to Emotional Healing

> *"Do not be anxious about anything instead, pray about everything. Tell God what you need, and thank him for all he has done. Then you will experience God's peace, which exceeds anything we can understand. His peace will guard your hearts and minds as you live in Christ Jesus."*
>
> *–Philippians 4:6-7*

What a promise is this! We just have to pray about our hurt, we just have to take our broken hearts to God, and he will replace our pain with peace. If the whole world knew this, wouldn't we be spending most of our time on our knees? It is a peace that transcends our understanding. That is a peace that sounds even stronger than your pain.

God wants you to use your emotional wounds to grow closer to Him. This doesn't mean that He orchestrated them to bring you in relationship with Him. In this world, bad things will happen and often they happen to good people. It grieves God too. But, if you let Him, He can work through your wounds to bring not only healing to your life but to the lives of others as well who you aren't even aware of right now.

In 2 Corinthians, Chapter 12, Christ says, "My grace is sufficient for you, for my power is made perfect in weakness." Paul goes on to write, "Therefore I will boast all the more gladly about my weakness so that Christ's power may rest on me..... For when I am weak, then I am strong."

When I finally understood what this verse meant it gave me chills. It does still. It doesn't mean that we glory in the midst of our pain, but that once we have learned to manage our pain and overcome its hold on us, we tell others that God was the reason. Why? We couldn't have gotten to the point of joy and victory if we hadn't surrendered the hurt to Him.

This is a paradox for many of us, because we all want to be strong. In God, we can be stronger than we can ever be alone. If our emotional suffering brings us closer to God, and as a result, makes us stronger, maybe our wounds are also blessings. We are all wounded healers in the service of the King. He can show you a purpose for your pain.

Acknowledging it All

What happens when we acknowledge something? If we are guilty, that means coming clean. It also means that we have to face up to the hurt and pain of the past. It can no longer be hidden. What possible benefit could that bring to us? For one, freedom is at stake. Take the first step and keep reading.

There is nothing new under the sun. King Solomon, in all his wisdom, said that in the book of Ecclesiastes. God has heard it all and seen even more. He can heal you but you have to give it all to Him.

As humans we tend to hold things back, fearing the look in people's eyes when they hear things about us: She was raped as a child; he was physically abused; they lived in a foster home; she came from a divorced home and never knew her father. It is all so painful and unfair. Why should others judge us?

Know this: God will never judge you. All He has ever wanted to do is love us and have us love and worship Him for the loving Father that He is. But, we tend to let shame drive a wedge between us and God even in our prayers.

You cannot change what you don't acknowledge or confront. When we are broken of spirit, the wounds of the past can overwhelm us and cause us pain and suffering, but God can heal our brokenness. He can't do this, however, if we don't first turn our hurts and sorrows over to Him.

You can shed your tears and bring your heart aches to Him and He will heal your broken heart and wounded spirit. He understands your tears and will give you the grace to not only carry on, but to triumph, all you have to do is turn to him with a contrite and willing heart. Ask God today to be the glue that binds the broken pieces of your shattered soul back together.

Dare to be vulnerable with God. If you are mad at your family for not helping you when you were being abused, tell God. If you felt angry because of the divorce, tell Him. If you have said hurtful words to others as a result of your pain and emotional suffering, let Him know all about it. He takes all emotional wounds without reservation.

Brokenness comes from holding on to our sorrows and letting them eat away at us. When we turn over those hurts to the Lord and ask Him to accept them, we have taken the first step toward healing.

You must admit that you've turned away from Him to concentrate on your own pain, and put forth a repentant and loving heart. Ask the Lord sincerely to take away your selfishness and your inability to turn from your sorrow and pain, and He will give you the strength and love to move beyond your past and step into a loving future in His presence.

Then, Trust God

Why is it so hard for us to trust? Well, most people prove untrustworthy. We are human. I can prove untrustworthy and so can you. But, there is One who will never fail to come through when you put your trust in Him. You've already taken the hardest step – admitting the pain and taking a good long look at it. Now, you are coming into the home stretch. Hold God's hand and you'll make it to the finish line.

When things happen in our lives that are upsetting or unfortunate, we sometimes say, God, where are you?" Things seem to be getting worse instead of better and we wonder why God allows bad things to happen to us. We have to keep in mind that God isn't punishing us or sending us trials or punishments – the world is filled with problems and troubles. God is still present in our lives to lift us up and give us hope despite the troubles of our daily lives. We simply have to let go and let God into the events of our lives so that everything can come together in the perfect order that He has planned for us.

> *"The Lord is good, a refuge in times of trouble. He cares for those who trust in him."*
>
> —*Nahum 1:7*

The next time you are suffering, whether it is because of some personal grief, a lost job, financial worries, illness or some other issue, don't ask God where He is. Keep in mind that God is *always* there for you. He is not the reason behind your suffering, but the One who will give you refuge and strength to see you through.

We all go through challenging times in our lives emotionally, financially, psychologically and spiritually. But we can trust in God to see us through. God is as close as the call of His name. No matter how low we've fallen or how depressed we are, God has the power to save our lives. Be willing to put your trust and faith in God; be willing to humble yourself and cry out to God for help from the depths of your heart and soul.

You may be asking yourself, "How do I know God can see me through *my* problem?" Remember, God has been here since the beginning of time and the world itself. From where we sit, our problems may seem insurmountable, but from where He sits as Ruler of the Universe, our problems aren't insurmountable at all. In fact, like a loving Father, He sees each of our problems and understands them. In His compassion and wisdom, He is simply waiting for you to come to Him and say, "Father, please help me to get through this. I *need* You."

If you want God to see you through, you must trust Him. And trust can be difficult when times are dark and life looks hopeless. Sometimes we want an easy fix and quick results. If our prayers aren't answered immediately, we wonder if God is really listening. Be faithful and understand that God, in His wisdom, knows what is best for you and that He knows what you have the strength to endure in the days ahead - and that He will always be with you. **Trust** in Him.

Turn to God in prayer and meditation and release your concerns about this day and the days ahead - turn them over to Him and He will help you to see them through. Just say, *"God, I trust you to be my guide and inspiration and to see me through whatever challenging circumstances I may have to face in the days ahead."* Finding your path to true emotional healing will not be without its ups and downs. In the Psalms, the Lord reminds us of just how much He loves us and how much He wants to be a part of our daily lives, seeing us through our daily struggles and being a part of our daily triumphs.

The Path to Emotional Healing

"The Lord says, "I will guide you along the best pathway for your life. I will advise you and watch over you"
—Psalm 32:8

Did God promise that the way would always be easy? No. But He did promise that He would always be there to guide you along the best path and watch over you. That's cause for happiness.

Move Towards Your Healing

There is a straight and righteous path to God's healing if we know the steps to take:

1. Actively seek God and His healing through prayer.

2. Confess that you are broken and that you are in need of His healing power.

3. Forgive yourself and others for whatever has happened. As long as you hold onto blame or anger, your brokenness will remain.

4. Let go of the bitterness and acknowledge that, no matter what has befallen you, you have something to be thankful for and happy about. This can be the most difficult step, especially if your loss has been a profound one. But as you pray to the Lord, He will remind you of the amazing gift that He has given you – eternal life and His unending

love! With these two great gifts, how can we hold onto our earthly pains?

5. Express your gratitude. Prayerfully thank the Lord for each day ahead of you that is a wealth of possibilities and the grace that grants you peace.

6. Remember that God has not burdened you with more than you can bear. You are still here! And with God's help you will rise from your knees with a stronger, steadier spirit than ever!

Prayer:

Heavenly Father,

Show me Your ways that I may walk with You. I surrender and give You every area of my heart.

Help me to acknowledge my pain, all of it. It has hidden me behind high walls all these years but has also made me a prisoner in my life. I don't want to be a prisoner anymore and suffer in silence.

Lead me to the doorway to your heart and help me to release my pain and brokenness to you. There is nothing you haven't heard before so I don't need to be ashamed to tell you about my pain and hurt.

The Path to Emotional Healing

Let me experience your unconditional and everlasting love as I lay at your feet, all that weighs heavy on my mind and my heart.

Help me to open up and let go, in faith, even though I am afraid. I choose to walk by faith and not by sight. Father, I trust You completely. You know the beginning from the end.

Thank you, Heavenly Father, for my healing and the purpose and promise that lay ahead for me through You.

In the Name of Jesus, Amen.

The Healing Power of Forgiveness

What does it mean to forgive? Some people can do it more readily than others. You may be thinking right now about the types of situations that would cause you to withhold your forgiveness from someone else. What about the situations in which you would forgive? How many times would you forgive? I wonder what God has to say about that?

Forgiveness will set you FREE. If you cannot let go and forgive those who have caused emotional pain in your life, then you are in bondage to the ones who have hurt you even though they may have moved on with their lives. Don't hang on to unforgiveness or bitterness. You punish yourself by not forgiving those who have hurt you.

I thank God for forgiveness. Without it, we wouldn't be able to come to Him without some sort of animal sacrifice like they did in the Bible days. It would be tough to reach God without a burning bush or a cloud of thunder.

God sacrificed His own son, Jesus, on the cross of Calvary to bring us this wonderful gift that knows no bounds. All that blood, pain, humiliation and tears were for us. As a result, His forgiveness is limitless.

One of the greatest gifts God gives to us is forgiveness. The reason it's such a magnificent gift is because it is such a wonderful and all-encompassing one- it covers all of our flaws and faults. When God forgives us, He does it whole-heartedly with no reservations or conditions, allowing us to heal from all of our hurts and sorrows. We don't have to earn his forgiveness or deserve it in some way - it simply washes over us from His full and loving heart!

God, Please Heal My Hurt and Unforgiveness

God's forgiveness washes away the hurt in our lives and helps us to heal from the bitterness and pain that may be lodged in our own hearts towards those who have hurt us or left us alone with their death. The hard part is passing that forgiveness on to other people - forgiveness is not easy for us, because we look around at those we need to forgive and we see that they have flaws or have made mistakes and we want to hold on to those past hurts and grievances. But that's where we're making a mistake - because *true* forgiveness, the forgiveness of God that truly comes from the heart, is a gift freely given to those who don't deserve it!

It's hard to grasp that concept when it is you who are in pain. All you can see is the faces of those who have hurt you but show no remorse. Why should they get off easy with our forgiveness? We want to hear an apology from them, so we hold our forgiveness for ransom until we get what we want.

The Healing Power of Forgiveness

But life doesn't work that way, at least with God it doesn't. We have made mistakes in our lives, too. Was there ever a time that you hurt someone else and were afraid to ask them for forgiveness? Maybe you thought they would close the door in your face or walk away from you or worse. So, you just kept away. To the person that you hurt, it probably seemed like you had no remorse in your heart for what you'd done.

It's easy to come to the wrong conclusions when we are carrying around hurt, anger and brokenness. Now, it's true that some people don't believe that they have done anything wrong when they cause pain in our lives. They feel justified in their actions and won't apologize for it. They are truly in need of the forgiveness that we can give.

When next you feel God's forgiveness washing over you, remember to take that next step and release those people in your life that have caused you pain or hurt. Allow your heart to forgive them and give them one of the greatest gifts there is to heal the human spirit.

It's easy to ask God to do things for us, but we can't forget that God also requires something of us - He wants us to treat others like we would want to be treated. How can we get down on our knees and ask Him to forgive us for all of our many sins and transgressions when we are so unwilling to let go of the mistakes and hurts that others have inflicted on us? God pardons all and we are to do the same.

The Path to Emotional Healing

There is a parable in the Bible that demonstrates this well. It is the Parable of the Unforgiving Servant in Matthew, chapter 18. A king had servants who owed him money. When he confronted the first servant he ordered that the man's family be sold to pay his debt. The man fell down on his knees and begged for mercy. The king, overcome with compassion, pardoned the servant.

Later on, that same servant met a fellow servant who owed him money. He wanted the full weight of the law to come down on that man for it. When the man begged for mercy, the servant refused and had the man thrown in prison. The other servants told the king who reminded the servant of the compassion that had been shown to him. For his harshness, the king had that same servant thrown in prison until he could pay also. The lack of forgiveness harms everyone's life.

Forgiveness is for you first and foremost, to begin experiencing God's healing. It is for others second so they can realize God's love through you and be forever changed. It is the first step towards healing hurt and pain.

God's love helps us to forgive. His forgiveness gives us the strength to turn toward others and express our own forgiveness, opening the way to a brighter future without rancor or grudges. It is truly forgiving and forgetting the wrong. We may not always have the opportunity to forgive someone in person, yet we can forgive then in our heart and mind, blessing them in our prayers.

6 Steps on How to Forgive Others

Pain stays with you until you release it. Use these six steps to help you arrive at the place where you can honestly forgive those who have hurt you.

1. **Talk to God first.** Let God know your pain. Tell Him that you are having trouble reaching that point where you can give up your anger. He will help you to realize that love covers a multitude of sins, like theirs and yours. Without forgiveness, your healing is in limbo and God's hands are tied.

2. **Read about Forgiveness.** The Bible has several passages on forgiveness. Through Jesus we learn that forgiveness is for all because of His sacrifice on the cross. In those passages is also a glimpse of God's love. Remember how God has pardoned you in the past.

3. **Release your Pain.** If you are looking for an apology, it may not come. Accepting that fact is hard but God will grant you peace about it if you simply ask Him. Within that peace that we know surpasses all human understanding, hand over your pain to Him. Tell Him everywhere it hurts and then let the pain slip into His hands.

4. **Thank God for What He is About to Do in Your Life.** When you finally let go of that pain, watch out. You are about to get the biggest blessing of all – a changed life. For so long you have lived like a prisoner chained to your

pain. It may not feel like you are free today, but then God is not about feelings. Keep thanking and praising Him until you believe with all your heart that you are free.

5. **Offer Your Forgiveness.** You can do this in person if you want to or if it is possible. Sometimes, the time has passed for making amends with another person because they are no longer with us. Even if they don't say a word, look them in the eyes and tell them that you forgive them for hurting you. It is not to hear them talking about their side, but instead listening to you. The situation is no longer about them, it is about you and God and your future life. If you can't be in their presence, lift up a prayer to God telling Him that you forgive that person in your heart.

6. **Live in that Forgiveness.** This is often another sticking point. The devil is crafty. He will try to get you to rehash that abuse in your mind. He will try to taunt you by telling you that you let the other person off easy. Don't buy it. When these thoughts come, go to God in prayer right away wherever you are. Once destructive thoughts take hold, it is hard to free yourself from them. The Holy Spirit will remind you of the love and the promise that God made to fix your broken pieces. Hold onto that promise no matter what.

Forgiving others is Christ's mandate because He has forgiven us so much. Forgiveness doesn't let the other person off the hook for what they have done. They have to seek their own forgiveness from God and themselves for that. What it does do is allow you to live a bountiful and blessed life in Christ because you are now once and for all, free from the pain.

Learning to Forgive Yourself

Through our hurt, we can continue the cycle of pain and brokenness. If you have been abused, you become the abuser when you don't confront your past emotional pain. Those hurting feelings become so ingrained that we allow our anger to be taken out on someone else who is innocent like we were. Sound familiar? If it does, you are not alone.

This occurs in many situations concerning emotional pain. If you lose a loved one, you refuse to accept love again in your life because you can't forgive yourself for surviving. Everyone who loves you is pushed away.

Pain begets more pain until everyone is hurting when you can't forgive yourself. Maybe you feel guilty because you couldn't stop what was happening to you whether it was a job loss, violent crime, abuse, accident or another situation. Deep down, you feel that maybe you are as much at fault as those who hurt you.

Now, you have continued to let it eat away at you and it has led to more suffering. So, not only do you have the pain of the original hurt on your shoulders but also pain that you have inflicted on others as a result. What an awful burden to carry around in your life for even one day!

It may be even more difficult to forgive ourselves than it is to forgive others. We often remember words we would like to take back or actions we regret years later or even minutes later. Through forgiving ourselves, we release the negativity and wasted energy we carry around and allow more positive, loving thoughts to fill our mind and heart.

Remember that God knows what is best for us. Isn't it presumptuous of us to think that He has forgiven us, but that we might know better than Him? After all, if we won't forgive ourselves, we are insinuating that we aren't deserving of forgiveness, despite God's opinion that we are. We don't accept His forgiveness, believing that He has made some sort of mistake. So let go of your self-hatred, pain and unforgiveness - you ARE worthy of self-forgiveness; God has already assured you of that!

There is no way to alter the past. When you look back in unforgiveness, you are cutting yourself off from the opportunities God is offering you for a real future based on His love and forgiveness. Let God forgive you and heal you - and allow yourself to forgive yourself and others who may have hurt you. Know that the pain and hurt will pass and God's promise for your life will be delivered. God has something special in mind for you.

> *"Do not judge, and you will not be judged; do not condemn, and you will not be condemned. Forgive, and you will be forgiven."*
>
> –Luke 6:37

This verse is also talking about when you judge yourself. You must forgive yourself for the mistakes you've made – and that can be a difficult thing to do. It's easy to try and hide our mistakes and not think about them, but what we hide has power over us. It can sit there in the back of our minds and fester, eating away at our self-assurance and our sense of God's love for us, making us wonder if we are truly worthy. We have to let go of our mistakes and forgive ourselves just as God forgives us each and every day. And He *does* forgive us – completely and with no reservations.

6 Steps towards Forgiving Yourself

There are six steps you can take that will help you in your struggle to let go of your past mistakes and embrace forgiveness. I've found these six steps very helpful in helping me on the path to self-forgiveness and closure.

1. **Acceptance and Ownership.** Accept and take ownership of your mistakes. Write your name on the top of a blank sheet of paper . Now take some time to think about all of those things you've never let go of in your past that you haven't forgiven yourself for. If you are still grieving a loss of any kind, you'll know many of those things right away.

Those nagging thoughts in your head that you are allowing to fester tell the whole story. Remember God is a god of comfort. He will NEVER condemn or trap you with your thoughts.

2. **Confirm your transgressions.** Write down your transgressions. Record what they are and who you hurt. If you hurt someone, then write down how you hurt them, etc. Was your hurt Addiction? Betrayal? Rejection? Theft? Lying? Financial? Dishonesty? Adultery? Pornography? Verbal or Physical Abuse? Emotional Abuse? Other hurt? God wants you to confess it all if you ever want to be totally free from it.

3. **Express your feelings.** Open your heart. Write down how you feel about yourself any past mistakes and unresolved feelings. Be very open and honest with yourself and God. Do you still feel unworthy after being forgiven by others or making amends ? God knows how you feel and He sees your heart. God also knows that you feel guilty about the pain inflicted upon you. Do you feel that you did something that made them hurt you? Abusers often tell their victims that they are just as responsible for the abuse to keep them silent about the crime. Express your feelings on paper and let your emotions flow freely – release them all!

4. **Decide to forgive yourself.** The power of forgiveness is not a feeling but a *decision* of the will. Forgiveness is one of the greatest gifts from God. God has told us to forgive

others, including ourselves and He has given us the power to do so – but it all begins with the *decision* of the will. When someone else hurts you, the guilt is theirs. Don't own it. When you have hurt others, God stands ready to forgive you and wash away your guilt because you have owned it. He has forgotten it and now, so should you.

5. **Acknowledgment and Prayer.** Acknowledge your forgiveness to God and take your transgression list to Him in prayer. You may have to spend some time reading and rereading your list until you are ready to go before your Heavenly Father. *"Lord, I come to You today and ask for forgiveness. Forgive me for all of my sins and I forgive myself. I forgive myself for _ (*list the transgressions that you have written down) _. *Ask God to heal your emotional wounds and help you move forward in the future without regrets and start fresh. Put all of your offenses into God's Hands. Release all of your past sins _ (*say them out loud) *_into God's Hands."* Now, believe God has forgiven you and sit a moment to bask in His grace and mercy.

6. **Emotional Closure.** Now is the time for your emotional closure. Destroy your transgression list in private. This visual and physical exercise can be very *freeing* emotionally. Whether you decide to shred it, burn it or tear up your list, imagine your past mistakes being permanently destroyed and disappearing in the same manner. As they disintegrate into smaller and smaller pieces until they are nothing that is how God has dealt with them also.

The Path to Emotional Healing

This is what it means to be "born again." The Lord doesn't want us to dwell on what has happened before – our lives as Christians are about who we are now and in the future, walking in forgiveness and love. So give yourself a wonderful gift that is free of charge and yet priceless – forgive yourself!

> *"Not that I have already obtained all this, or have already been made perfect, but I press on to take hold of that for which Christ Jesus took hold of me. Brothers, I do not consider myself yet to have taken hold of it. But one thing I do: Forgetting what is behind and straining toward what is ahead, I press on toward the goal to win the prize for which God has called me heavenward in Christ Jesus."*
> –Philippians 3:12-14

Prayer:

Heavenly Father,

Every moment with You is precious.

In this moment of meditation and prayer, I release any unresolved feelings of anger, resentment or regret in my life. I release to You any unresolved feelings that I have toward myself.

Help me through this process of emotional healing.

The Healing Power of Forgiveness

Forgive me for any pain and hurt that I have caused in the lives of others. Forgive me for not letting go of the past and moving forward in love and faith.

I experience now the emotional healing power of your forgiveness to the depths of my being.

Heavenly Father, I acknowledge and give thanks for Your everlasting and unconditional love that strengthens me, comforts and soothes me emotionally, mentally, physically and spiritually.

Thank you for healing my heart and bringing Joy , Meaning and Peace back into my life. Thank you, Heavenly Father, for forgiving me and setting me FREE.

In the Name of Jesus, Amen.

This is a new beginning releasing the past and embracing forgiveness. Forgiveness opens the door to the enrichment of all our relationships so that they flourish with understanding and love. With the forgiveness you express today, you open the way to a brighter future.

Choose to Be Free from Your Past

We all have a past. When today is gone, what you did will be in the past. Will it inspire good memories or bad ones? The decision is up to you. And that leads to another important point – cutting the pain and hurt of the past out of your life is also up to you. Do you want to continue to sacrifice your happiness for it? I didn't think so. Well, God has the tools you need to cut away the excess baggage.

I don't know many people who live entirely without regrets. Unless you've been blessed with a significant bump on the head, you, too, probably carry around memories that you'd rather forget. No one has lived a sainted life, which makes God's forgiveness, grace and mercy all the sweeter when we receive it. But it is up to us to decide whether we will strain our muscles dragging that baggage around or whether we'll unpack our issues and deal with them. (We can always repack, right?)

In Chapter 8 of the Book of John, Jesus was teaching in the temple courts, and some teachers brought in a woman who had been caught cheating on her husband. They made her stand in front of everyone and they said to Jesus, "Teacher, this woman was caught in the act of adultery. In the Law,

Moses commanded us to stone such women. Now what do you say?"

Have you ever felt condemned for something you've done like this woman? It might not be adultery. However, we all have felt condemned for something. I know I have. Not that anyone has ever attempted to stone me, thank God, but I've had metaphorical rocks hurled at me plenty of times. Do you know what Jesus said to her accusers? He said, "If any one of you is without sin, let him be the first to throw a stone at her."

I guess that those men must have put some thought into Jesus' words because they wandered off without a word. The woman stood where she was, until Jesus stood up and said to her, "Woman, where are they? Has no one condemned you?" "No one, sir," she said. "Then neither do I condemn you," Jesus declared. "Go now and leave your life of sin."

There are many lessons to be taken from this simple, yet powerful story. First of all, Jesus calls the teachers out as if He were saying: "Hey, we all have a past. We all have issues. Every one of you has something you'd rather not share." We make our own decisions in life, right or wrong. If we live well, we will learn from those mistakes and, by the grace of God, come out on the other side without too many dings and dents. If there were sinless people on earth, then Christ would not have needed to die.

Choose to Be Free from Your Past

Secondly, Jesus tells the unnamed woman, "I do not condemn you." This might not have meant as much to her then as it does to us now. We don't know whether or not she was aware that she was receiving a pardon from God Himself. She was fine not to have been killed that day. But we can look at this scene and know that Christ was saying to this woman, "I am not judging you, go on now, get on with your life, and stop cheating on your husband."

Thirdly, Jesus met this woman at the level of her need. This is so important in the lives of those who don't yet believe in Him. He could have been like the teachers and used the letter of the law to get rid of the woman while letting the man involved go free. It would have suited their purpose to let her die. She wasn't obeying the law.

You'll see it over and over with Jesus. When He met the tax collector, the woman at the well and those that some thought to be of low station, He didn't spout laws and commandments. He dealt with where they were at the moment, first. If someone offers to give you bread when you are hungry, you will, more than likely, sit and listen to whatever else they have to say.

God offers us forgiveness for our past, no questions asked. He does tell us, like Jesus told the woman, to go and stop sinning so we can enjoy a life of peace with Him.

Can this apply to any mistakes we've made in our pasts? Christ sacrificed Himself on the cross so that we could be forgiven our sins. If we wallow in unnecessary, harmful guilt, then we are not fully accepting His sacrifice, His selfless gift. We are acting as if Jesus' sacrifice meant nothing at all.

If He wanted us to feel guilty, to spend time, and muscle power, dragging that baggage around, He wouldn't have made the ultimate sacrifice. He gave His life, in a brutal fashion, to buy our freedom – freedom from sin, freedom from death and freedom from our own pasts. Later on in this same chapter, Christ says, "Then you will know the truth, and the truth will set you free." Jesus Christ is this Truth.

So, you're asking, what about those of us who have suffered due to no fault of our own? Yes, that happens in life also. Painful things certainly happen to innocent people. We live in a fallen world that is counting down. Victims of disease, oppression, rape, child abuse, adultery, the list goes on. Life is not fair.

God doesn't want you to live with the ghosts of the awful things that happen to you all your life even if it is not your fault. He sent Jesus to earth so that we might have a more abundant life than we had without Him. If you feel trapped by the circumstances of your past, then you need Him right now. It's the only way to truly be happy again.

Accept Christ through Faith

People aren't the accepting type. We often try to make deals and bargain to keep from getting what we don't want. In regards to past pain and future happiness, by not accepting the path that God reveals, results in further pain. Christ is the path. Follow Him and learn how to obtain your happiness starting today. Exercise your faith.

Anyone who knows the story of the Cross thinks that Jesus Christ was strong and faced His suffering head on. If you read carefully, you'll see that in the Garden of Gethsemane, He agonized over the coming pain and suffering. He asked God if there was another way besides pain to complete His mission. In the silence, He turned His eyes towards heaven and told His Father that IF there wasn't, He would do as God had asked. Wow!

Faith is easier said than done. It is difficult for those who have truly suffered to believe that their suffering can lead to a greater purpose. In the Book of Ephesians, chapter 1, verse 11, the Apostle Paul writes, "In him we are also chosen, having been predestined according to the plan of him who works out everything in conformity with the purpose of his will."

Believers are chosen by God. Sometimes, when we are suffering, or when we have suffered, we wish we hadn't been chosen, but the truth is, it feels good to be chosen, especially when we are able and willing to believe that our suffering, our pain, is going to work out for the purpose of His will.

Unfortunately, we don't always know when we are suffering that this is what is happening. You may have suffered as a child and have struggled to make sense of it all your life. There can be a significant amount of time between your suffering stage and your understanding stage. God has a different sense of timing than we do.

But, rest assured, He has a way of making all things work together for our good. It says so in Romans 8:28. God is love. God's Will leads to love, even if there are some unlovely bumps in the road along the way.

Writer George Bernard Shaw wrote, "If you can't get rid of the skeleton in your closet, you might as well teach it to dance." This is an apt metaphor for creativity, and that's how this quote is usually interpreted, but it also reminds me of God's Will. The phrase is not meant to trivialize anyone's pain but it gives us a different perspective on it.

Oftentimes, we are able to use our past, our mistakes, or our time spent as innocent victims, to love and instruct others and to glorify God. Recovering alcoholics can minister to those struggling with alcoholism. Ex-convicts can minister in the jails. Rape victims can counsel other rape victims. Abuse victims can use their story of trial and triumph to bring others out of the darkness of their experience and into the light of God's love.

Suffering is difficult; there are no bones about that. But we need to know that God is not judging us. Psalm 103 reads, "As far as the east is from the west, so far has he removed our transgressions from us." That's a long way – that's infinity! God has forgiven us. In light of His sacrifice, it is the least that we can do to forgive ourselves. He has also asked us to use everything in our power for His glory.

Find Emotional Freedom and Closure

Is it possible to use your past to bless others? Is this the way to truly be free of it?

When there is no closure in our lives, we continue to hurt long after the moment that first caused us pain has passed. When we are troubled by past transgressions we can't forget, our lives continue to be an open wound that can't heal. We become "walking wounded" wearing masks and can't get on with our lives. We feel incomplete and unfinished, as though something in our lives is lacking.

How do you find closure after death, separation, divorce, or the pain of a parent who doesn't love you? What do you do to find peace when your life continues to show the scars of past abuse or terrible loss?

God will soothe your soul and help bring you peace if only you will lay your sorrows and anger at His feet. Sometimes it's hard to go to the Lord and confess how angry we are at a loved one because of a past slight or some terrible harm they caused us. After all, we want to be good Christians and forgive – but if there is still pain in our hearts, it can be difficult to do.

It is also difficult to go to God with angry feelings about a loved one who has died and left us alone in the world. It seems selfish since they are the ones who have lost their lives, but we can't always control how we feel about a situation. That is why we need God to help us to sort everything out, because pain and grief don't make sense to us.

Closure is the final chapter on the past. You timidly recognized your pain and met it at the door instead of shutting the door in its face. It was hard, but God helped you greet it and deal with it. Every hurt feeling and thought is thrown at him so that he can take it back. God is there to assure you that He has heard it all before so don't hold back on His account.

Through prayer (lots of it), reading God's Word, and learning about forgiveness, you learned that God's love can overcome any pain. He wants you to forgive those who hurt you and yourself for any hurts you caused because forgiveness is the key to future abundant life and freedom. It isn't easy to reach this point, especially if you have decided to confront the person who hurt you and offer that forgiveness.

Managing your grief can come down to accepting forgiveness for yourself. As long as there is something of that pain left, it will never leave you alone. It's like that visitor at the door leaving his hat behind when you show him out. If something of his is left behind then he can always come back to visit. With emotional pain, you don't want any repeat visits. When he leaves, he takes everything he owns with him.

> *"Give all your worries and cares to God, for He cares about you."*
>
> *–1 Peter 5:7*

After doing all of that, it is time to move forward. Staying in the same place is not the next step after letting go of emotional pain. It's time to start fresh and find your happy life. Find that place that God has prepared for you already, but He was just waiting for you to take hold of it. Take your life back by finding the door, shutting it and never looking back, except to tell others how you made it over.

Final closure can be found in writing a letter to God. This step can be beneficial to those who don't have an actual person physically available to forgive or tell them what they feel. But, even if you do, you are spending time with God, telling Him how you have felt – the good, the guilt and the ugly.

Writing down what is eating at your soul can help you move past it. We hate to rant and rave at God when we pray, shouting about how bitter or disappointed we are; it seems so disrespectful. But God *wants* to hear everything in our hearts

— even the ugly stuff. So sit down tonight and write a letter to God. It might look like this:

"Dear God,
I'm so angry! I hate my husband for betraying me, and I can't get past it. I wish he would just go away and leave me alone forever….."

Once you start writing, you will find that all of the bitterness, hurt and sorrow will come spilling out and onto the page. That's good! It's very cleansing to finally admit, even to yourself, that you have been hanging on to unfinished business and letting yourself dwell on the past.

After you've written your letter, make it a sacrifice to God, for even our pain, when given with a true and faithful heart, is a gift to our Lord. He will take the sorrow you've written about and soothe it away for you. Some people may even want to burn or shred the letter after they've asked God to help them find closure. It is a simple ritual that can give you a feeling of release – you have admitted what the problem is, asked God to help you move forward, and now you can let it go! Once you've done this, you will feel a sense of peace and happiness as the closure you've been seeking for so long finds its place in your heart!

This is important for mending relationships especially after a crisis. If you've pushed everyone away in word or deed, welcome them back and share your story of healing with them. All too often, tragedy or the revelation of a long held secret can tear families apart. God will be the cement that reshape your relationships and hold you together tightly.

So, what will you do now? Allow the light of God to shine through you in all that you do. Through the power and presence of God, you are free to realize your divine potential. Everyone has one. Live as the free and resourceful person God originally created you to be. Demonstrate the abilities you knew you had (but were obscured by your past) and discover even more. Live in an awareness of oneness with God.

Discovering Your Divine Purpose Leads to Happiness

If you could ask God one question most of all, would it be, "What's my purpose in life?" Nothing matters more than knowing God's purpose for your life. It is what you were created to do. Think about it.

Let go of preconceived notions. In this way, you won't be disappointed and you also will remain open to what God has for you to do on His behalf. Think of it this way: You can do anything that God sets before you. He is the master of everything. Who knows what you might get to do?

Have you ever heard someone say that God didn't give them any spiritual gifts or talents? That is like when a little kid tries to show you their bicep and then says that they don't have any muscles yet. Your gifts and talents are there; they may not be developed yet. Part of discovering your divine purpose and living a happier life is learning what treasures God has hidden within you and how you are supposed to use them.

Discovering the divine gifts can seem overwhelming. After all, there is no instruction manual, or is there? You guessed it: the Bible is our instruction manual for living a successful Christian life. Within its pages are the keys to unlock your God-given gifts and talents.

We are made by God and made for Him. Discovering your divine purpose leads to a successful life filled with joy, peace and happiness – precious fruits of God's tree. God has placed the potential for greatness (in His eyes) in all of us. This is not bright lights and red carpets like in Hollywood but the love and approval of your Heavenly Father who rules all. If He knows your name, then you truly are special!

To harness this potential, we have to identify it, develop it and utilize it so we can be a blessing to humanity. Each one of us is filled with divine potential awaiting discovery. Divine potential is our untapped "God energy" that helps us to reach God's highest good for our lives. You are more than what you see in the mirror each day (as stunning as that image may be!) you are what God sees: His precious gift born with unlimited divine power.

Can God lead You to Self-Discovery?

Self-discovery takes courage. Do you have that? If you have overcome difficulties in your life (such as abuse and addiction) can you help others to achieve what you have? It would mean talking about the past, but as one who has met and defeated their past, not as a victim-*but as a victor*. Your story is one of *victory*. God might be leading you along this path. Will you go?

Discovering Your Divine Purpose Leads to Happiness

There are hundreds of self-help books on the shelves today about self-awareness or self-discovery. More people take time off every year from their normal lives so that they can "find themselves." In fact, it has even become somewhat of a joke that people going through a mid-life crisis are trying to find themselves – as though they misplaced who they are!

But it isn't always a joke. True self-discovery is crucial to being comfortable in our own skins and is a key element of being a successful Christian. God wants us to understand ourselves, not in a selfish way, but in the sense that we must understand our place in His creation and His plan if we are to be fully appreciative of Him. We can't know God without knowing ourselves, because we are His children!

Through the ages, many people have recognized this need and prayed for the ability to understand themselves better. St. Augustine asked God to guide him toward self-discovery centuries ago:

> *"Grant, Lord, that I may know myself that I may know Thee."*

Self-discovery is about learning not only who you are, but what part you hold in God's plan. He didn't create you in order to simply take up space! He has a purpose especially for you, and until you go on the journey of self-discovery, you can't understand what your role is. That doesn't mean that you can't make dreams of your own. In fact, when you are young and deciding what to do with your life, many of your hopes and dreams come from talents and gifts given to you by God even though you weren't aware of that fact at the time.

You may already be working through those talents, but it wasn't for God. When God comes into your life and guides your path, He shows you how those same things you are doing can be magnified to give Him greater glory and you an even more abundant life. Our first and foremost goal is His glory so more people can learn about Him and believe in Him.

> "And I, if I be lifted up from the earth, will draw all men unto me."
>
> –John 12:32

Jesus was talking about His death on the Cross, but every believer carries that sacrifice inside of them when they accept Him as their Lord and Savior. When people see God working through us (our gifts and talents), they see Him and want to get to know more about Him.

After all, how can you fulfill the destiny God has for you unless you know what gifts you can use to achieve that destiny? Just as important is the flip side of self-discovery – awareness of your faults. Knowing what causes you to stumble and fall is crucial to success in any endeavor, but never more so than when you are seeking God. There is nothing wrong with having shortcomings. Everyone is not good at everything. It is then that we rely just a little more on God to see us through.

So self-discovery goes both ways – God can help you achieve it, and the more self-aware you are, the closer you can draw to God. How wonderful that God has created this unique dynamic for us!

Ask God Questions to Discover Your True Self

God will always be there when we come to Him with questions. He wants us to ask questions so that He can give us the right answers and guide us in the right paths, so don't be afraid to ask when you're seeking your true self.

* *Why am I here?*
* *What do you want me to do with my life?*
* *What do you want me to learn?*
* *How do I overcome my fears, self-doubts and insecurities?*
* *What steps do I need to take to further understand myself and God?*

All of the questions above can be taken to God in prayer. Whenever you talk to God, you learn a bit more about yourself. You can discover ways to overcome your flaws when you lay them down before Him. You can understand better how to use the gifts He has given you and will be able to manage them better.

When you begin the journey of self-discovery through God, never be afraid of what you find out about yourself! God made you distinctive for a reason! Finding out what that reason is and following the plan God has for you is the greatest form of self-discovery there is.

How to Discover Your Divine Life's Purpose

These seven steps will help you on your journey to discovering your reason for being. This is an important step in many lives that have been full of emotional pain and grief. You may not have realized that there was a brighter and bolder side to life but now you will. These steps are only guidelines. Let God lead you from one to the other (in the order that pleases Him) as you open your heart and mind to Him.

1. **Pray and Read the Word**- Make a God connection. God knows your purpose. He knows what you were put here on earth to do. Have a heart to heart conversation with God. God will help you to understand what His words in the Bible mean.

    Get yourself a version of the Bible that suits you. The King James version is not for everyone. God doesn't want you to be frustrated just trying to figure out what the literal meaning of the words is. You may also need a concordance, to look up passages that may be familiar to you from earlier life but you only know a few words. A Bible dictionary helps you to understand the meaning of words

Discovering Your Divine Purpose Leads to Happiness

as they were used during biblical times. Reading God's word is study time with the Father, your teacher. Come prepared to learn about Him and yourself; then, pray for understanding.

2. **Learn to love yourself.** It will result in a better understanding of who you are. You cannot find your life purpose from God if you lack self-love. After all, God is love. Negative thoughts you have developed about yourself will mask your true identity. These thoughts can lead to sadness, depression, feeling hopeless and anger at yourself and the world. Some of them may have been the result of a shattered past or the unkind words of others when you made mistakes.

   By adopting positive reinforcement techniques, you can learn to let go of that self-hate mentality. You are not who the world says you are but who God says you are. Look at yourself through His eyes. Ask Him to show you how. Once you release all of the anger and pain, a whole new world of hope will unfold. Take time to relax and meditate. Ask yourself what makes you unique. Focus on what inspires you and what makes you happy. God may also reveal the answers to you through other people in your life.

3. **Sit in a comfortable and quiet place without any distractions.** Get a pen and paper and make a list of what you believe your natural gifts are (you will go through a lot of paper in this exercise). For instance, what are your talents?

What do you do that comes naturally to you? What have you done in the past that was meaningful and gave you a sense of accomplishment? It can be something very small or big. The key is to write as many meaningful talents that you can think of. Listen to your answers. You may find that in no time, you will have a very impressive list. Here are some examples: great planner, very creative, knows how to cook well, learns new tasks fast, has an outgoing personality, makes friends easily, is a good listener, and et cetera.

Here are some life purpose questions for you to answer:

- What do you love to do?
- What are you naturally good at? (skills, gifts, abilities, etc.)
- What would you do with your talent or passion if money was no object?
- What makes you smile?
- What makes you feel great about yourself?
- What causes do you strongly believe in?
- What do people seek your advice about or help in?
- What would you do if you knew you could not fail at it?
- What do people compliment you on?

Discovering Your Divine Purpose Leads to Happiness

- What are some hardships, difficulties or challenges you have had to overcome? Would you be willing to help others with those same challenges?

One way to discover your spiritual gifts (which the Holy Spirit gives to each believer), is through reading the Word. There are several passages in the Bible that speak directly about what some of the spiritual gifts are: Romans 12:4-8, 1 Corinthians 12.

You can also pick up a spiritual gifts inventory. You can find them online by typing in the keywords "spiritual gifts inventory." Your church Bible study leader may have one. Some churches give them to new members to help them learn about where God wants them to serve, just like we are doing now.

4. **Find Your Passion.** A passion is something that you feel strongly about and are committed to, like God. Let's say that you have a passion for helping other people. Make a list of all of the times that you have helped others. At first, you may think you have never helped anyone. This is because you are thinking too big. Remember, helping others does not only mean helping a large number of people. For instance, have you ever placed a food item in a drop-off box for a charity that feeds homeless people?

   You may think one item is not a big contribution, however to that one person who eats the food you donated, it means a lot to him or her. It means the hunger pains will go away. You have made a difference in one person's life.

You did something that was meaningful. You did it without expecting something in return. You performed a selfless act and you should give yourself a hug.

A passion makes you happy. When you are working within a talent or gift (that is where your passion stems from), you are at peace. That is the kind of happiness anyone would want. You are totally consumed by what you are doing in that moment. Ask others what they think you are passionate about. Ask God to send you confirmation of your passion.

5. **Make a list of all of the important people in your life.** Part of how we define ourselves is by how we think others see us. For each person, write down what you think they feel is your purpose in life. Try to imagine what they think of you. You will soon find that what you have written is not what they think necessarily (unless you asked them), but they are expectations you have created for yourself.

Think about these expectations. Do they seem excessive or unrealistic? Before long, you will discover that you are carrying a lot of unnecessary weight that you need to release. We often see ourselves as we think others want us to be and that may not necessarily be the calling you were created for. Let those pre-conceived notions about yourself drop to the floor. Once you take off the self-imposed emotional shackles that have been weighing you down,

Discovering Your Divine Purpose Leads to Happiness

you will be one step closer to finding your true life's purpose.

6. **Ask yourself some important questions.** Once your spirit is lighter, you will be able to ask yourself such questions as: What makes you feel passionate? What makes you smile? What makes you feel alive inside? When do you feel proud (not in a haughty way)? You can ask and answer these questions better now because the negative thoughts have been exchanged for positive, self-affirming language and you can see a much clearer picture. You have learned to look inwardly instead of externally to find the answers to your deepest and most personal questions. If you're still having trouble, ask God for more help.

7. **Write down your life purpose.** Once you have removed the negative thoughts, perceptions, and external influences, you will have a much clearer path to discovering your life purpose. Your internal compass will be readjusted as your thinking becomes much clearer. Write down a clear and meaningful life purpose statement that echoes personal meaning based on your internal self. Don't force it. With all of the knowledge about yourself that you have accumulated, go to God in prayer and ask Him to reveal it to you. It will emerge naturally and will bring great joy and a sense of peace. Then, ask God in prayer for confirmation.

I know that you are ready to move on with your life and live abundantly, but discovering your life purpose won't necessarily happen overnight. God is able to do anything, but the truth is in the journey and so are the faith and the grace of God. Give yourself time to make your discovery just as you gave yourself time to heal.

Speaking Positive Life-Changing Words

Your positive words prophesy what you become. When you change your words you change your life. Talk the way you want to be and you will become the words you speak. Make your words count.

The words we speak help create our world and our experiences. The words we speak are powerful enough to bring results. If we speak positive words, we will get positive results and if we speak negative words we get negative results. Use your words to speak emotional healing over your life. You have what you say.

Most of the time, we are thinking negative thoughts without even realizing it. If you have been through a devastating time in your life, it is natural to think that it will last forever. In light of that struggle, you begin a self-fulfilling prophesy for your life.

What's that? A self-fulfilling prophecy is one that you speak into existence. God told us that we our words could either loosen His hands to pour out blessings or tie them behind His back. That is why it is so important to trust God in all areas of our lives.

That simple act of faith releases Him to further increase our faith and trust with evidence: a friend who calls just when we needed someone to talk to, a confirming word from a church member about our talent as a Sunday school teacher or that still small voice that whispered "I am here," as you prayed for emotional healing.

Negative words are meant to hold you down and bind you up. You have already experienced bondage in the form of emotional brokenness. You don't want to go there again. But, the mind is the key.

The Importance of Words

Words are important. Whether spoken or written, men and women throughout the ages have been taught well or ill of because of them.

The Bible talks about words. God spoke the words and the world was born. Nothing existed until he spoke.

Our lives are similar to the creation of the world. What are you speaking into your life? Will it help you or hinder you?

In the book of Proverbs, there is a scripture that tells us the tongue holds the power of life and death. That is a powerful statement. Think about evil World Leaders for a moment. People are executed with a single word that falls from their lips.

Speaking Positive Life-Changing Words

You may not be a World Leader, but your words have the power to affect the same type of change in your own life. You can change your life for the better or the worse with what you say.

The words that we speak and there power are directly proportional to our faith. If you remember your math classes in high school, when something is directly proportional, both parts increase or decrease at the same time. If you lack faith, your words will lack power. If you have faith, you can move mountains with your words.

Each of us has read at least one self help book. The reader changes their way of thinking to change their circumstances. One way they do this is through words. The more you repeat a phrase, the more you will come to believe what you are saying.

This method has helped many people. Equally, for as many as have been helped, there are others who just couldn't make it work. There was something that was lacking – faith.

Now, true faith comes through Jesus Christ. Faith in man is not faith at all because it is fleeting. Jesus is different. When the going gets tough for us, He is still that strong hand at our back giving us the strength to go on.

It is upon that faith, that we use our words to change our lives. Speaking positive words can bring positive results in our lives, WHEN God is the source of our faith. Jesus told His disciples that they could wither the fig tree as He did or move mountains with their unwavering words grounded in faith.

The Path to Emotional Healing

Try an experiment. Ask God for something, anything. It could be that your car gets fixed even though you know you don't have the money right now. Or, ask for a renewed relationship with your spouse after things have gone bad.

These are what we call "mountains." Jesus said that our words will move them. Speak positive words into each of these mountains. After you ask God for these things, do not speak negatively about them again.

When you think of them, speak the Word of God instead. How do you do that? Quote Bible verses that reflect what God has said about speaking positively. Let Christ's mind be in you. That gives your words power. As you speak the Bible verses keep believing, keep hoping and keep standing on God's word because the answer is on the way. God always keeps His promises.

Repeat God's words back to Him *out loud*. Here is an example: Father, You said, "Listen to me ! You can pray for anything and if you believe you will have it"- Mark 11:24. I am standing on Your word that my marriage will be restored according to Your will, In Jesus Name, Amen. *Say it until you see your blessing manifest.* Use this example and fill-in-the-blank with your situation or problem and select a powerful Bible verse or verses that relate to the problem. Embrace the promises God has in store for you.

> "*Every word of God proves true*".
>
> –*Proverbs 30:5*

Through that power, you will receive your blessing. It is important to note that God is not a genie. You may not get an answer today or tomorrow, but your faith will grow stronger through patient waiting. Wait on God's perfect timing- *for the right outcome.*

On the other hand, negative words can reflect a lack of faith or a lack of knowledge. As a new creation in Christ, you have the same power as Jesus. You can ask the Father for what you want, according to His will and you will receive it.

As you grow in your knowledge of God and your faith, those negative words will fall away and be replaced with positive life-changing words filled with God's power. Your word power is the architect of your future.

A War is being Waged

Did you know that a war is going on for your very soul in your mind? Think back to the self-fulfilling prophecy. Have you ever gone somewhere that you weren't sure you wanted to go and by the time you got there you had talked yourself out of staying? You just pulled up, turned around and went back home.

We've all done it once or twice, just like we talked ourselves into that favorite junk food we didn't need (but that's another story). Whatever you think and dream, you can achieve in your life. The Word of God says that we are to take captive every thought and make it obedient to Christ (2 Corinthians 10:5). This means that any thought that contradicts what the Word of God says is to be removed from our minds.

When you tell yourself that you are a failure and worthless, that is a lie. When you say that God doesn't love you because of your past, which is another bold lie. Don't take my word for it. The Word of God says so:

> *"This is love: not that we loved God, but that he loved us and sent his Son as an atoning sacrifice for our sins."*
> *−1 John 4:10*

So, all of those times you tell yourself that you are no good or damaged goods are nonsense. God made you and He is not a junk dealer. You are made in the image of the Almighty God. There is nothing damaged about you.

Changing your words is hard, but you can do it with God's help. You have already learned to go from pain and bondage to joy and freedom at the beginning of this book. The last holdout is usually your words. Unless you take the time to realize what you are saying and how damaging it can be, your freedom will only be temporary.

Having an Attitude of Gratitude

Changing your thought patterns is the first step. Is there a reason for me to be thankful today? If you are alive to read

Speaking Positive Life-Changing Words

the question, then you have a reason for rejoicing! It may not always seem that way when troubles press in on you, but as long as you are alive, you have the opportunity to change your life and move forward.

One of the most important gifts of all is life, and it was given to you by the Lord. Sometimes we forget the generosity of a loving God. After all, He doesn't need us and did not have to create us in the first place. Yet He wished to share His blessings and so created man in His own image so that He could shower man with love. Even when man first betrayed God in the Garden of Eden, God continued to love and protect mankind. He forgave us our faults and sent His only son, Jesus Christ, to give us guidance and grant us forgiveness! And God continues to do this, even though we often forget to be grateful for His kindness.

Now think back over recent months. Have you lived in gratitude? Have you remembered and acknowledged God's grace and goodwill in your life? It's easy to forget our many blessings when we are stressed or grieved, but we need to re-evaluate our lives during these moments.

When your job stresses you out, give thanks to God that you are employed. When your children talk back, praise God for giving you healthy children. When you are going through a painful separation or quarrel, remember that God is there for you, and take comfort in knowing that He is there to pull you through.

It doesn't seem to make sense to the human brain, but you are developing a grateful spirit. When you can see the good that God is doing even in the worst of times, you learn to understand how He thinks. Ask God to help you see through your spiritual eyes.

> *"And let the peace of Christ rule in your hearts, to which indeed you were called in the one body. And be thankful."*
>
> *–Colossians 3:15*

When we have an attitude of gratitude, we soon discover that we attract greater good in our lives. Be grateful for all of the good that the Lord has granted you, and you will soon reap even greater blessings. Giving thanks to God for all of the many daily blessings in your life – shelter, food, your senses, friends and family – opens your heart to all the good you have and enables you to appreciate life.

Sharing those blessings and being grateful for them brings you closer to God. When you draw near to Him, He will draw near to you and you will learn His ways and adopt them instead of the negative thinking the world had reduced you to.

> *"Yours, O Lord, is the greatness and power*
> *and the glory and majesty and the splendor,*
> *for everything in heaven and earth is yours…*
> *In your hands are strength and power*
> *To exalt and give strength to all.*

Speaking Positive Life-Changing Words

Now, our God, we give you thanks,
And praise your glorious name."
—1 Chronicles 29:11-13

So as you move through your days and weeks, keep your eyes on the goodness of God and recognize that He has, in His generosity and love, given you far more than anyone else can ever give you. Find the blessings in every situation and you will develop an attitude of gratitude for the many physical, material, emotional and spiritual blessings that have been given by God, the source of all good in our lives. Each day, show your gratitude to God and thank Him with all your heart. Your life will be transformed one thought at a time.

Celebrate Your Uniqueness

There will never be another human on this earth just like you. Celebrate yourself for the special being that you are. This is not a selfish or egotistical act in the least. By taking the time to stop and appreciate who you are and what you have to offer, you are, in essence, thanking God for His indescribable gift.

You have already begun to learn about the plan and purpose God has for you locked away in that limitless divine potential. Each one of us makes up a part of God's body – the church. This is not a physical building but the body of Christ composed of those who believe in Him. We come from all walks of life but we are one in Him. No one else can do what God created you to do. If you don't do it, then someone is going to miss a blessing.

So, how can you honor that uniqueness? Here are a few ways.

1. **Thank God for every part of you.** None of us is perfect. And, in good human fashion, we will always have one thing (maybe two) about ourselves that we wish we could change. Even if you want to lose a few pounds (everyone talks about weight these days) thank God that you can exercise or that He provides you with the healthy foods you need to get the job done.

2. **Create self-affirmations.** These are not mantras, but scriptures that support the good things that you think about yourself. Here's an example: *God says in His word that I am "wonderfully and fearfully made." That means that God took care to make me. I am loved.*

3. **Speak the Word of God.** It's okay to use common adages like "This too shall pass" and "You'll make it through," but there is no power behind those words. God said that His word has power. Let the Word of the Lord speak for you. Recite powerful verses such as, *"I can do all things through Christ who strengthens me"-Philippians 4:13*, *"The Lord is my shepherd, I shall not want"- Psalm 23:1*, *"Commit to the Lord whatever you do, and your plans will succeed"-Proverbs 16:3*, that will release God's power. Ask God for the supernatural power He offers. Faith is your connection to God's power.

4. **Tell your story.** No one else knows what God has done for you. Enlighten them with God's goodness towards you.

The Power of Your Testimony

In a courtroom, testimony is given by witnesses. Those witnesses tell the story of what happened and what they know as they experienced it. They tell a story that they believe is true, and they testify in order to help others understand what happened. As Christians, we have a testimony of our own to

Celebrate Your Uniqueness

give – the story of the power of God's love and the miracles He has worked in your lives.

But how many of us actually take the time to witness to others? When is the last time you gave your testimony about God's presence in your life? You should tell your story whenever the opportunity presents itself because it will give God the Glory He deserves and it will encourage and inspire those who hear it.

The power of individual testimony shouldn't be underestimated. If a friend or co-worker is having a rough time, take the time to listen and give them a shoulder to cry on. But don't stop there – let them know you are praying for them and that God loves them. When others see that your life is blessed by confidence, love and God's presence, they will want to know more.

You can give your testimony a number of ways. You can tell your story, dividing it into "BC," for Before Christ's presence and "AC," for After Christ entered your life. Reveal your feelings of hopelessness and loneliness before Christ entered your heart, and then talk about the fulfillment, strength and sense of purpose you've discovered with God.

Think back on what you have shared with your friends and family in the past months. Have you told others about a good book you enjoyed? How about a great movie that you encourage them to see? How often have you talked about your relationship with God? After all, we know what is important in someone's life by what they talk about.

Your uncle talks constantly about his passion for vintage cars, your best friend talks a lot about her fiancé and your sister loves talking about shopping. Yet how often do we talk about the God we love and who loves us? If you love God, talk about Him! Share the good news with others around you.

Every time we testify to God's grace and love, we are opening up an opportunity for others to discover God. And with God's love bringing us joy and peace, we are increasing our own happiness by sharing it. Showing God's love to others is contagious – the more we share, the more others will receive and it will be passed on. What a wonderful way to praise the Lord! Let your light as God's child shine in both word and deed.

> *"You are the light of the world. A city on a hill cannot be hidden. Neither do people light a lamp and put it under a bowl. Instead they put it on a stand and it gives light to everyone in the house. In the same way, let your light shine before men, that they may see your good deeds and praise your Father in heaven."*
> —Matthew 5:13-16

So the next time you are talking to others about what is important in your life, don't forget to give God the glory He deserves. You will not only please Him, you may open a door

Celebrate Your Uniqueness

for someone else to explore the Lord's blessings. The power of your testimony may be what brings a lost and hurting soul to God. There's no greater "thank you" that you can give Him than this, because He's seeking his lost sheep even today.

Yes, your testimony makes you unique. God sends us to those He wants us to talk to. Your words can make the difference between life and death for someone else.

The Power of Giving

What you make happen for others, God will make happen for you. Giving back can change your life.

What brings you happiness? Usually we think of things that center around ourselves: Eating a fine meal, meeting with friends, sharing time with family. All of these situations enhance our feelings about ourselves. But, what about those who we don't know?

Have you ever helped someone across the street? Smiled at a person for no reason other than to share a bit of humanity? How about giving the shopper in front of you some money so that they can buy their groceries? If you did these things or something similar, how did it make you feel? Giving is another aspect of lifelong happiness.

All you have to do is watch the news to realize that the world is in turmoil. People are suffering all over the place. The point here is not that they are suffering. Emotional healing is needed because of suffering that we have faced. The really distressing thing is that they are facing their suffering without God.

What can you do about it? Here we are not talking about just prayer (which is a powerful tool in itself), we are talking about being hearers and "doers" of the Word (James 1:22). God tells us to take care of the poor and the widow. Jesus showed us throughout the Gospels how He demonstrated the Father's command to "love one another." We have learned throughout this book that we are to be "wounded healers" for God.

It is time to step up and get going in the lives of those in your communities and in your own church family. If you don't have a church family, ask God to lead you to one that is a good fit for who He is molding you to be.

Giving is personal and powerful. Jesus demonstrated that when He washed the feet of His disciples. At first they weren't having it, but then He told them that they were no part of Him if they didn't. Afterwards, He told them to do the same for others. We are all the same in the eyes of God, because He created us. That means there is no job too big or small for you to do for His kingdom.

Where are your talents and gifts needed? Serve at the soup kitchen to help others get a hot meal. Donate your good clothing that you don't need to an agency that will distribute them to those in need. Help a stranger reach that can of vegetables on the top shelf in the grocery store. When God lays it on your heart to intervene on someone else's behalf, do it even if you think they will look at you strangely. God is leading you to give of yourself or something you have and there is no mistaking that. Get creative and "throw the box away"(don't just think out of the box) to reach the unchurched and churched. Ask God for creative ideas and ways to meet the needs of the people you are in contact with everyday.

How do we know where to give? For the most part, it's simple. God gave a command to love others. If you see someone in need and you can help, do so.

Other times, God has specific things He wants us to do or say to another. This requires that we have a "good ear" as we listen for His voice and commands. If you are not sure, you can always ask Him.

Sometimes the answers we seek reveal themselves immediately, while at other times they come at a time and in a manner that's unexpected and disconcerting. We may struggle against what the answer is, but God's love for us is patient – He will keep offering His answers and wait for us to listen. He won't abandon us if we refuse to hear the first time or even the tenth time! You see, God loves us so much that He is willing to give us the answers over and over until we are ready to receive them.

There will be times where we give until it hurts. If you are called to share your past with another, this may be the case. We won't always want to do what God asks, but like I said, He is patient and will keep telling us the same thing over and over until we accept it. And, hopefully, the next time, we will listen on the first go round.

But how do we learn to truly listen and accept God's answers for our lives? First, we must realize that listening so that we truly *hear* God's call is the most important thing in our lives. If we are too busy with the hustle and hurry of our everyday lives, we may not hear because God's voice is drowned out by the world's confusion. You must set aside time to *listen* and *hear*.

Giving sets the stage for God to enter someone else's heart. It softens that hard exterior so He can make an appearance, through you. There is no greater honor than winning souls for the Savior. The Bible says it makes you "wise."

These simple steps will help you open up to what God wants to say:

1. Train yourself to hear the Lord by reading your Bible, which is the Word of God. His Word will open your heart and your ears to the sound of His voice and His desire for you.

2. Look for and listen to God's words in the world around you. As you open your heart, you will be amazed by the many signs of God's love for you that surround you even in the gravest of circumstances.

3. Give yourself over to God's will. You may hear the word of God and be afraid of what He has planned for you and you may want to turn away – but ignoring God's plan when you have heard it is worse than never having heard

it at all. The most important part of hearing is truly *listening to* God! And listening requires a heart and soul that are ready to receive God wholeheartedly.

Are you ready to listen to God? Then talk to Him and open your heart so that it is ready when God speaks to you!

> *"Listen to advice and accept instruction, that you may gain wisdom for the future."*
> *– Proverbs 19:20*

Happiness is an Inside Job

Happiness is a result of what you believe and what you do, not a result of what happens to you. In God's world, this type of happiness is called "joy." Do you have joy in your life?

We all too often focus on the appearance of the outside of ourselves. We beautify the part that people can see. But, did you know that the parts you can't see influence how the parts that you can see will look? Think of it this way: If you don't eat enough food, your body will begin to look thin and gaunt on the outside (undesirable). Conversely, if you eat too much, you will begin to balloon on the outside (equally undesirable).

The same goes for your spiritual and mental well-being. How you take care of the inside will show on the outside. By the way, how is that inside job going? What can be done to bring you close to a life of happiness?

How do you get joy down inside of you? It's not easy, but it's worth the effort. Joy is one of the Fruits of the Spirit (Galatians 5: 22-23). These are attributes that God develops in us through the Holy Spirit as we grow as a Christian. They start small, like most fruit do and grow in abundance with the right nutrition: prayer, Bible study, and fellowshipping with others, trials and tribulations.

All of these fruits have there start on the inside before they are ever revealed to the world, much like apples that begin as flowers and then turn into fruit. So, your happiness, or joy, begins with God working on the inside of you.

Love from the Inside Out

Most of us think that if we could just get a better job, meet the right person, buy that gorgeous house…or something else we're longing for, we will be happy. We think that once we've achieved some concrete goal or obtained a certain amount of money, we will be happy; but we can be very disappointed when we find out that the recognition or the money don't give us the happiness we wanted.

The circumstances you are in aren't nearly as important as how you *respond* to those circumstances. If you respond with prayer and a sincere desire to love Him and your fellow man despite bad circumstances, you will discover that God gives you the skills you need to overcome your circumstances or be happy *despite* them. Trusting in God, opening yourself to new possibilities and giving of your person to others will lead to true happiness. God's love and love for yourself (which naturally lead to happiness) are perfected in loving others. He's made it easy for us to find happiness by trying to make others happy. What a wonderful plan – we increase our joy by bringing joy to others!

Happiness is an Inside Job

"So I concluded that there is nothing better for people than to be happy and to enjoy themselves as long as they can."

– Ecclesiastes 3:12

God understands that the material things and the praise of others isn't what will make us happy. That's why He doesn't always grant our wishes right away. He's working on our insides first because He knows that what matters is what is in our heart and soul. God focuses on the real source of happiness – our relationship with Him – so that we will be happy with ourselves and ready to handle the good and the bad that life hands us.

Are you happy with yourself? If not, no amount of money and no change in your circumstances will change things. You have to learn to *love yourself like God loves you.* When you can do this, you will be happy within your own skin, and the rest of your life will fall into place more easily. Turn yourself over to God body, heart and soul and you will be amazed – He never leaves us the way He found us! He is always working on us, healing old wounds and restoring our faith. As He does this, you will find yourself increasingly seeking to do what is right and good in His eyes – and you'll discover the joy of a Christian life.

Begin working today on getting to know and love God and you will soon know yourself better, love yourself and understand yourself. Allow God to work on your insides and you will be healed of the disappointments and hurt in your life – and room will open up in your soul for true happiness. Ask God to work on you from the inside out so that you will become the person He has always meant you to be and you will find happiness in His purpose for you. Give God control and let Him mold you as He sees fit. Surrender yourself and find happiness in God's plan.

> *"'For I know the plans I have for you,' declares the Lord, 'plans to prosper you and not to harm you, plans to give you hope and a future.'"*
> —Jeremiah 29:11

Who we are on the inside has everything to do with what our lives look like on the outside.

Daily Affirmation

Speak aloud or silently this affirmation as truth and inspiration throughout each day of your life. Give thanks in advance for God's guidance, power and protection over your life.

Affirm Your New Path

God Loves Me,
God is Guiding Me,
God is Protecting Me,
God is Showing Me How to Live a Life of Happiness.

Be Happy Living How

What if the doctor told you that you had only one year to live? How would you act? What would you do? What would be the most important things you would want to accomplish? What will you do with the gifts, talents, and relationships God has given you? More importantly, what would you say about your life: *Did I live happy? Did I love? Did I make a difference? Did I live my purpose?*

Wouldn't it be nice if there was an easy way to guarantee happiness? So many of us find ourselves thinking, "If only I had a decent job/special someone/more money I would be happy." Unfortunately, once we get the thing we've most desired, we often find that the happiness we thought it would bring doesn't appear.

That's because happiness comes from the *inside,* not something external. No one can "make" us happy. It comes from being comfortable with whom you are and understanding and embracing the choices we make in life. Are you content with whom you are becoming? Happiness is a choice and a way of life.

Many people waste their lives in the pursuit of false happiness: drinking, using drugs and pursuing money or relationships that are outside of God' law. They soon find that these are simply temporary Band-Aids and not genuine paths to happiness. They might temporarily cover up your unhappiness, grief and sadness, but they won't lead to lasting joy. Perhaps true happiness means something more than living in the moment! You can start living happy now not just for the moment but every day.

Don't put off your happiness and dreams until tomorrow. Life is short. I know it sounds like a cliché that people use, but it is true. Look around you. We live in a violent world that snuffs out the life of young and old alike. Live happy now and with purpose. Focus on your dreams and goals.

Live happy now while you are still in your living years . There will come a day when you won't have the physical energy or stamina to go after your goals. It will be hard to run around the world on mission trips when you are 90 years old. The mind begins to slow down as well. So, maximize your time here on earth now by making every day count.

We can be poor judges of what will make us happy. Our lives, without God, are proof of that. Divorce, depression, loss of self-esteem, anger and grief: all of these run roughshod over our lives. Why? Because we tried methods that we *thought* would make us happy and turn things around but it didn't. But if we follow God's path, putting our trust in Him, we will discover happiness right close by, if we want it.

There are Five Principles for Achieving Your Goals:

1. **Clear Vision** – The clearer your vision for happiness, health and prosperity (true spiritual wealth), the faster you move toward it and the faster it moves towards you. Create a vision for yourself for the long-term future. When you can see the mental picture, the more positive, more focused, more motivated and more determine you will be in achieving your goals and living a life of happiness and purpose.

2. **Develop a Smart Strategy** – Write down your goals and be specific. Take out a sheet of paper and write "Goals" at the top. Make a list of everything you can think of that you want to accomplish. Organize the list in order of importance and timeframe (when you will accomplish your goals) and then develop a plan of action to achieve each and every one of them. Amazing things happen when you write down your goals and believe they will become reality in your life.

3. **Intense Determination** – You will need to develop strength of mind and heart for this one. Here is a question to ask and answer over and over again throughout your life: If you were guaranteed success, pursuing any goal in life large or small , short-term or long-term, what would it be? What goals would you pursue if you knew you could not fail? Go after every goal with this mindset and objective.

4. **Protect Your Focus** – Identify and eliminate any self-sabotaging behaviors in your life: Fear, anxiety, poor time management, lack of discipline or concentration. Protect your focus. It determines your reality. Choose to live a happy life now.

5. **Create a Powerful Support Team** – Surround yourself with people who believe in you and support your vision. Build your winning team with positive , ethical, loyal, talented, skilled, goal-oriented and success-driven people that want you to achieve the best out of life. It is essential that your friends and supporters will be people who will tell you the truth and have a prayer life. True friends and supporters will add and multiply to your life. The opposite of true friends and supporters are those that subtract and divide from your life. Give the following profound quote some thought as it relates to having the *extra eyes* of true friends and supporters, "It is hard to *see* the picture when you are in the frame". True friends and supporters will always see things in us and opportunities that we aren't able to see. They will speak the truth over our lives. We might not like hearing the *truth* sometimes. However, they will always have our best interest at *heart*. Ask God in prayer to send the "right" people that will support you in every area of your life. Just ask and He will send the very best.

"Seek his will in all you do, and he will direct your paths."
                                                                    –Proverbs 3:6

Be Happy Living How

To live happy now and achieve your goals requires faith and belief in yourself, positive attitude, integrity, vision, hard work, desire, determination and dedication. All things are possible for those who believe in God. Take your power back. Decide how you want to live, act and feel. Love yourself and be happy now and pursue your dreams and goals with passion and purpose. Enjoy your journey. You are *God's very best*.

One Final Thought

You know how you feel something with every fiber of your being and search for a way to help others understand just how important that "something" is to you? That is how I feel about helping others to help God meet them at the level of their need. In the case of this book, the need is emotional healing.

It can, no; it IS devastating to experience pain in your life. It doesn't matter if that pain is due to a death, abuse at the hands of another, a sketchy past or a physical problem. When we feel hurt, it is real to God.

You are very valuable to God. God loves you so much. He accepts and loves you unconditionally. The influences of the world may have gotten you to doubt that, but it is time to find out who is really telling the truth. Hurting people can hurt others. Those that doubt Him haven't understood the loving God I know.

We don't always know why pain and suffering comes into our lives. The one thing that we do know is that God is not hurting us. He is just as grieved as we are when we are hurt by another. He never meant for His children to be so vicious to one another. But, we all have free will and sadly, many turn against Him and go their own way. I'm sure you know that leading a life away from God can lead you to do some desperate things you aren't proud of hence the sketchy past you don't want others to know about.

It can seem like we suffer in silence, with no word from on high. God has His reasons for that and we have explored some of them. As we endure, He is with us always.

Instead of pointing a finger at God, put your hand out to Him. I guarantee that He will take it into His and wipe the pain away. The Word of God says that He gives us "beauty for ashes." Whatever we go through, He will return to us "double for our trouble."

Nothing is forever, except God's love. It will stand the test of time until eternity. Let God have your pain so that you can spend eternity by His side.

Walk in faith, love, joy, peace and victory. With God you can be emotionally healed and go on living the life that God meant for you to live. Your best days are ahead of you. God sees the best in **YOU!**

About the Author

Robert Moment is a personal growth "throw the box away" in-demand inspirational life coach, speaker and author of several books. Robert specializes in maximizing human potential by bringing out the best in individuals to help them find their purpose and live a life of true happiness and success.

Robert is passionate about empowering individuals on how to experience God's love, peace, power, joy and prosperity (true spiritual wealth) in their lives. Operate in the fullness of God's Plan for Your Life.

Experience Life-Changing Power...

Visit his websites:
    www.HowToBeHappyAgain.com
    www.ChristianInspirational.org

Contact Robert for Speaking and Workshop Opportunities:
    Email: Robert@HowToBeHappyAgain.com

More Information
    This book is available for bulk sale. To inquire about pricing for twenty or more copies (sold at a substantial discount, non-returnable), please send an email message to:
    discount@HowToBeHappyAgain.com

www.ingramcontent.com/pod-product-compliance
Lightning Source LLC
Chambersburg PA
CBHW071717040426
42446CB00011B/2098